MY THIRD HALF

ED PHELAN, FSC

Published by Ed Phelan, FSC, in 2021.

phelane@gmail.com

EdPhelan.com

On the cover: At the De La Salle
Christian Brothers Training Center in
1958 and again in 1983,
altogether a view of three halves of life.

Dedicated to my friend
Charles Kitson, FSC
1949 - 2016

CONTENTS

BEING & DOING

"You don't always have to be doing something.
You can just be, and that's plenty."
- Alice Walker

For many years I thought there were two
halves of life. I discovered otherwise.

In the first part, we prepare for our life's work, decide on
a profession, earn a reputation, hang lots of diplomas on the
wall, settle down, and nurture family—a lot of *doing*.

In the next, we contribute to the world, refine our reputation,
move up in the organization, welcome the next generation of
the family, and prepare to move on—a lot more *doing*.
Then one day . . . Eureka! I discovered a third half—retirement.

It is the time to discover the wisdom of years, start replacing
the diplomas, look into my deepest self, bless and praise the
next generation, show kindness, love the God within,
and so much more—less *doing* and more *being*.

For the longest time I have considered
being and **doing** as opposite ends of a spectrum
of my life—the mutually exclusive either/or choices.

Recently, I have come to understand being
and doing in nondual terms much like the ancient
Chinese philosophers described the Yin Yang.

For them, and now for me, seemingly opposite
or contrary forces may actually be complementary,
interconnected, and give rise to each other
as they interrelate.

The yin-yang symbolizes that sense of
oneness emerging in my third half and serves
as the thread that holds these chapters together.

My Third Half Becoming

For 25 years in the company of over 100
staff members, I helped strong and connected families
build personal and social assets and collaborate
in community change. It was excellent preparation
for the third half of my life.

In 2007, when I realized at age 67 that the time had come for me to retire.

I was the Executive Director of the Highbridge Community Life Center, a community-based organization in the South Bronx, and I had no idea what awaited me in the years ahead.

Young and gifted, I was impressed by some good men at La Salle Academy and wanted to follow them.

I knew that my 25 years in that position would not make an easy transition for either the organization or myself. Therefore, I accepted the help of a foundation-supported transition consultant, a move that made all the difference and enabled the organization to create an organic change without its services suffering. I could see the positive effects of executive transition for the agency, and it minimized the guilty feeling I had in leaving the organization after so many years. It was the end of the second half of my life.

I considered my years at Highbridge as the continuation of a call I have felt all my life to help vulnerable families be healthy and connected. I trace the origin of that call back to a whisper I heard in the 1950s as a high school student at La Salle Academy on the Lower East Side of Manhattan.

I admired many of the Christian Brothers who taught me—they were authentic human beings who exhibited deep care and concern for us students and our families.

In 1958, I officially committed
to joining the Christian Brothers.

That's me on the top row, 2nd from right.

They belonged to a religious order in the Catholic Church, the De La Salle Christian Brothers, and lived together as a community next to the school. I decided I wanted to be one of them. And it felt good. I was moving from the outside to the inside of this remarkable group.

With Mom and Dad as I began my journey

After an initial year of retreat and reflection near Redhook, New York, I attended Catholic University in Washington, DC. In 1963, at age 23, I was assigned to teach and live in the South Bronx (known to the US government as the poorest congressional district in our country).

Before long, with a Ph.D. in hand, I became the school principal. A group of school parents soon invited me to establish an adult education center, and in just a few years, it became a BA-level college program for adult residents of the Bronx. I became the Campus Director of over 1,000 adult students. It may have been the most impoverished neighborhood by federal standards but it was one of the richest in committed and connected families.

Over time, I moved from a concern for me to a sense of us. I felt I belonged in that place. For 20 years, I worked very hard, earned many diplomas, moved many ideas from rhetoric to reality, got promotions, slept little, survived the darkest days of the South Bronx, and learned to listen to neighborhood families. I had moved from a career to a calling. It was the first half of my life.

Finally, at age 43, I was able to bring all that I learned in the first half of life to the Highbridge neighborhood of the Bronx. That would last for 25 years. Highbridge helped healthy and connected families through services in adult basic education, family counseling, community organizing, after-school tutoring, and homeless outreach. In the face of the AIDS epidemic, we converted the abandoned, historic Home of the Friendless in Highbridge into a large residence for persons with AIDS.

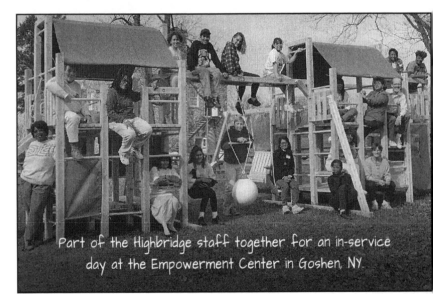

Part of the Highbridge staff together for an in-service day at the Empowerment Center in Goshen, NY.

Another project of those years was establishing the Empowerment Center in Goshen, NY. It's a place of rest, relaxation, learning, and renewal for the families. It was an abandoned schoolhouse brought back to life with the help of the Sisters of St. Dominic, the owners, and the weekend labor of Highbridge residents.

I loved being part of the Highbridge Community Life Center. I had become a leader with a strong feeling of co-responsibility alongside my colleagues and community residents who worked to advance the Highbridge neighborhood.

It was the second half of my life.

For both halves of my life, family has inspired me to be my best. Our family has lived in various locations near our work and has included a few other Christian Brothers like myself and young women and men committed to a year or two of service. In this intentional community/family, we Brothers have tended to be older and more permanent members, balanced by those young women and men who recently graduated from college.

These young Lasallian Volunteers—who I have lived with for 20 years by the time of my retirement—continue to capture my heart. They are generous men and women who want to give back skills they received by helping the children and their families of the South Bronx. Many even go on to careers in service, inspired by their time with the Lasallian mission.

I love the youthful excitement and energy they broadcast. I think I saw in them the life I wanted in me. Our community of older Brothers and younger volunteers became a family who cared for each other, cried together, and challenged each other to be the best version of ourselves. And it has continued to this day. We pray, cook, share our lives and become lifelong friends.

Care and support are palpable for each of us and felt by the many guests we regularly host. Over the years, several

Just one iteration of our Bronx family
with symbols of our mission.

refugees have joined us until they could get their bearings in our city by obtaining work and improving their English.

It is the compassionate presence found so often in families. They are the link between the first half, the second half, and what I call the third half of my life—retirement.

Personally, this family living has afforded me endless opportunities for generativity—that is, the chance to make a difference in a person's life through affirmation, communication, love, and affection. The response I have often received has sustained my life and fueled an inner joy deep in my heart. It has helped me be my best in retirement.

Sensitivity and intuition are essential guardrails for me to keep my interactions focused on our family members' needs and not merely on my own. I am the "grandpa" our younger members might not have had—and I love it.

Our young volunteers moved me from thinking that Brothers share their mission with laymen and women who staff Lasallian schools and programs to realizing that every individual shares the same mission of Jesus to bring people to the Father. As time goes on, these Brothers pass the torch to their younger partners.

Sharing community with volunteers and Brothers in the Bronx has opened my eyes to an international phenomenon of community. Similar groups to ours have sprung up in many other countries. If this trend continues, I have no fear for the future of Lasallian shared communities and the mission they proclaim. These future Lasallians will be recruited by the evident

What we love most
about our
HOME
is who we
SHARE
it with.

Our Bronx family in 2010 at a Lasallian workshop.

needs of massive numbers of children and their parents in every country of the world.

Being involved in helping other humans do better in any way works magic on the human soul. Young sixth graders in the Bronx did it for me. This helping relationship is built into the human condition. Once a person gets touched by this relationship in our Lasallian Family, he or she is often caught for life. Friends often remind family members of all the good they do for children and families—but truth be told, the latter are helping Lasallians even more to realize their call in life. With a little time and reflection, these Lasallians realize one of my favorite expressions: "meeting human needs is evangelical."

In more traditional terms, all these women and men share in a vocation or a heartfelt response to vulnerable families' needs and to the God who calls through them. Initially, this vocation is felt from within and soon links them with many others as a family—the Lasallian Family, named after De La Salle, a creative 17th-century French gentleman turned priest turned mission-starter.

Often a common realization for these Lasallians is they are not alone in their mission, rather they are near other like-minded family members. Mutual respect and acceptance on a local level grow, and before long small groups develop common objectives. A sense of community and faith sharing often inspires a small group of local leaders in what they call a ministry.

With heartfelt reflection and years of experience, Lasallians grow spiritually into the understanding that their call is first and foremost from the God who loves them unreservedly. It is a call to discipleship. They are in love with God and driven to bring about the reign of God in our world. Their vocation is a Divine calling for the good of an ever-expanding world community.

In my retirement years since 2008, I have seen a significant increase in the numbers of women and men Lasallians who are Lifelong Lasallians, permanent members of the family. This amazing development is happening simultaneously as the number of active Brothers is diminishing in most areas of the world. The result is a net gain of Lasallians who can meet the need and continue the mission.

Some call this change "passing the torch" to our partners, but it is simply family growth to meet expanded needs.

We journey as a family on pilgrimage. It is a movement. All share the charism; that is, the push from the Spirit of God for people's service.

Some live intentionally with other Lasallians as we do in the Bronx, while most of our expanded family are part of nonresidential communities. Some are young. Some are old. Some are married. Others are single. Some are committed for now, and some forever.

All realize that change is a constant on this journey and a sign of God alive with us. We respect the divinity in ourselves and all people as we champion issues such as ecological sustainability, just policies, immigration, social justice, fair distribution of wealth, racial justice, non-violence, and women's rights.

In recent years, members of this family have become the frontline workers and leaders across the US and beyond. Those are the Lifelong Lasallians.

The contributions of so many women and men partners have inspired me and other Lasallians who attended a Rome

The formation program in Rome where I met Monique Ayeyi, a Lasallian teacher from the Gulf of Benin in West Africa. Others represented 35 different countries.

formation program in 2019 called *Great Things are Possible: Lasallian Association for the Future.* The program highlighted the importance of Lifelong Lasallians for the mission's future. Several of us participants decided to invite this pivotal group in our region to self-identify, speak on their own behalf, and help us all look ahead to a future under their leadership. I invited them to plan a manifesto of the future and form a Lifelong Lasallian Circle of Partners.

Soon after we began, the Covid-19 pandemic struck and caused delays in the process, but at the right moment, I feel they will emerge and organize.

Chris Giangregorio ★ Lifelong Lasallian

Several years ago, on visiting De Marillac Academy (a Lasallian middle school in the Tenderloin neighborhood of San Francisco) I met Chris Giangregorio on the front steps as he greeted every student by name, a firm handshake, and a word of welcome. The school is one of about a dozen others in the San Miguel tradition addressing the needs of junior high boys in underserved neighborhoods of major cities. Classes are small, days are extended, and summer programs guarantee yearlong learning. They are very student-centered.

Chris coordinating with Lasallian Volunteers

After graduation from college, Chris was personally converted by this approach to teaching and learning as a Lasallian Volunteer in Harlem, New York. The Resurrection School had eager students, supportive parents, and professional, experienced staff. Chris was ready to learn and help in any way he could. Chris drove the bus, shoveled snow off the sidewalk, coached basketball (he is 6'3"), shopped for the community, and taught sixth-grade math. He was a team player who learned the power of working together with parents, students, and fellow teachers—something Lasallians call "association." He understood good management practice and leadership skills.

It is not surprising that he became the principal of De Marillac Academy and continued his professional studies in management at St. Mary's College in Moraga, CA. Today, Chris holds the position of Principal and CEO at De La Salle Academy, a San Miguel School in Concord, CA.

Chris was initially introduced to the Lasallian Family in Harlem. On June 14, 2008, he and fellow former Lasallian Volunteer Kristen Corbal married and started their own family.

Earlier in life, these exceptional individuals entered the Lasallian Family via different doors: some planned this move for some time, some were simply searching for employment, and others found the needs of the children and vulnerable families pulling on their hearts like a mysterious call.

With time, all of these good people were captured by the Lasallian mission and were often invited to participate in local formation or national programs (like the Lasallian Leadership Institute, the Buttimer Institute, the John Johnston Institute, or Lasallian Social Justice Institute). The Spirit has been at work in their lives.

For many years, these dedicated women and men studied all the Lasallian documents, the chapters, and De La Salle's writings, all to understand better the meaning of being Lasallian in our world. As time went on, they realized that they were and are protagonists in this family. They are De La Salle for our world—they are the Christ redeeming all of creation.

Today, they find themselves somewhat steeped in this Lasallian spirit and feel a daily call to continue in the mission. They work and live and move together with others on this Lasallian journey. Their sense of connectedness with each other further cements the feeling of being a Lifelong Lasallian. They grow in the realization that they are helping to bring about the Reign of God in our world, and the title

"Lifelong" has more to do with their daily dedication to the mission than their longevity in service to the mission.

The head of the Lasallian family and his council in Circular 461 identified ways these men and women have embedded themselves in different cultures in Christian and multi-religious forms. It is time for Lasallians to speak on their behalf, take their leadership role in the family in proportion to their numbers and sex, recruit and train their successors, and do the work of the Spirit in our world. They are now the mind, heart, and soul of the Lasallian mission in the world today.

I am proud of this Lasallian Family's global spread and honored to affirm and support the thousands of men and women frontline workers worldwide.

Retirement has afforded me the luxury of time and attention I need to "see" what is happening. It is another way of "being" in our world.

Over the years of the first and second half of life, I had a keen sense of becoming older and wiser. At the same time, I was becoming less impressed with power, position, influence, and more taken with becoming a more authentic human being—the task of the third half.

Heather Ruple Gilson ★ Lifelong Lasallian

Heather met many Miguel Men in her Providence, Rhode Island, sixth-grade classroom and her life was changed forever. Many of those eleven-year-olds were children of vulnerable, immigrant families and all of them were eager to learn from this new teacher. As a Lasallian Volunteer, she was a member of the Manton Ave Lasallian Community by night and a member of the San Miguel School Community by day.

Heather and me in Rome for an international Lasallian workshop

The call of those young men captivated her heart for another ten years as a teacher, counselor, coach, and academic dean. She gradually realized meeting their needs to learn and mature was her vocation in life. She was bringing about the reign of God in this world. The boys called her to her lifelong mission.

Heather moved along in the Lasallian Family and headed back to her native California to manage an extensive program for Lasallian youth, and chaired the Lasallian Volunteer Advisory Board for several years.. After marrying fellow Lasallian Joe Gilson (from Malta) in 2015, the couple moved to just outside of London and started a family. Both continue their Lasallian mission with the Lasallian Family of England and Ireland. In addition, she is the Co-Secretary for Association at the International Lasallian Center in Rome. Heather is a Lifelong Lasallian.

PART I

Doing
in the
Third Half

My Third Half is filled
with opportunities to grow
and DO some good for others.
It is a process of becoming,
living out what I
<u>was</u> meant to be.

I accept being retired.

I affirm the whole Lasallian Family's
efforts to help vulnerable families.

I encourage the Lasallian body politic
to continue to apply its thriving spirit or
charism to our modern world's needs,
and listen carefully to the women of our family
and to the feminine residing within us.

*In the Yin Yang, the latter
stands for light, day, authority
and outward energy . . .
the **DOING** of my retirement.*

20

1

Accepting the Fact

Eight years after retiring, a group of students
at Manhattan College invited me to share my
faith and life journey with them and participate
in a group sharing . . . a challenging invitation
seldom received in my life.

January 1, 2008, marked my retirement from Highbridge and the beginning of my slow understanding of the third half of life—and I would like to emphasize the word "slow."

A group of students at Manhattan College invited me to be a guest speaker in the fall of 2016 at one of their Agape Latte evening discussions. They wanted me to share my faith and life journey with them and participate in a group sharing, a challenging invitation seldom received in my life.

I felt vulnerable and humbled at this sort of sharing. Vulnerable because I shared a hidden, tender part of myself with strangers. Humbled that they wanted to learn more about me.

After considerable thought and some prayer, I entitled my comments "Daring Greatly to Help: One Surprise After Another."

I self-identified at the time as a 76 year old De La Salle Christian Brother; a member of an intentional Lasallian community of eight men and women; a resident and worker for many years in a neglected neighborhood of the Bronx; and a leader and manager in innovative education and community development programs, always ready to dare to help in meeting surprise after surprise in life. It was my first and second half of life in 15 minutes.

By the end of the rich discussion that followed my presentation, I learned a valuable lesson about myself that has stayed with me ever since—I discussed Highbridge Community Life Center, never in my remarks did I say I had retired from that organization almost eight years earlier. Hence, most of their questions were directed toward a full-time executive director of a not-for-profit agency in the Bronx of 2016—something I hadn't been in eight years. I realized I had unintentionally neglected to simply state that "I retired on January 1, 2008."

I faced what retirement meant to me at that point—namely, the end of something good, the loss of a meaningful mission, the diminution of power and influence. For most of my adult life, I had enormous energy for work, high motivation for results, determination to overcome obstacles, and a strong desire to change the world. Unconsciously, I feared all this had ended in retirement. What would I do now?

In almost any application for getting an account, applying for a workshop, signing up for a course, or purchasing an airline ticket, we are asked many questions. Among the usual questions of name, address, email, and phone number, one other stands out for me in the third half of life—position.

What position did I currently hold? I paid little attention to this question for the first and second half of my life as a teacher, principal, program director, executive director, Auxiliary Visitor, and Director of Senior Brothers.

Nowadays, I stop for a few seconds to decide what my "position" is, in much the same way I hesitate on "date" when I am not sure. "Retired" comes to mind first, but it does not answer the position question. Not long ago, I responded with "human" and, on another occasion, "alive." I've even left it blank because this question typically lacks an asterisk.

It is another way our culture tends to underline the importance of a person's position over all other possible characteristics a person might have. For me, it is a routine reminder of the importance of all that I am and do beyond any specific position. Perhaps in the future, I might simply say my role in life is observer, affirmer, challenger, model, or inspirer.

In the days that followed my presentation at Manhattan College, I could feel change welling up from inside me. It was a call to put aside the temptation Richard Rohr calls "regressive restoration of persona," the desire for things to be as they were in the past. I hoped to embrace the fact I was in retirement for several years already, and I needed to look upon my life differently. I could not live in the past but could only understand and love where I was at the time. It occurred to me that I was in a particular season of my life, different from the earlier ones. Like the other stages before it, this one called me to embrace it.

I realized a formidable enemy was merely lethargy.

At the time, I realized a formidable enemy was merely lethargy.

Often, retired people know they can not "be" and "do" as earlier in life. The challenge becomes learning to embrace their "being" over much of their "doing." It is the inner spirit that we can easily neglect earlier in life. Being unwilling to go deep nurtures the lethargy of retirement. It's a low level depression that can paralyze good people in retirement. It often seems that the more successful a person's career had been earlier in life, the greater the temptation to lethargy in retirement.

Beyond individuals, this same lethargy can affect groups and organizations, especially those who have been very successful in the past and whose members' median age is close to retirement. Their past success blinds them to meet the needs of the current world.

As we move from
one half to another,
there are plenty of
constants to keep us
grounded, like our home
for the Lasallian
community of
Bedford Park
on Marion Avenue
in the Bronx.

Carl Jung would call this resistance in individuals and organizations their shadow. I see this in the wider Christian Brothers' organization. They have a glorious history of helping youth and their families for over 300 years, and many see little reason to adjust and retool in our changing world.

The median age of our Brothers in the US hovers near 75. The organization's challenge is the same as it was for me facing retirement—the fear of seizing the moment and taking risks for the sake of carrying on the charism.

As a group, we need to step back and listen to the call of our modern world.

The call comes through people.

In each stage, I had been invited or called by people. Seldom did I ever turn down their invitation. It was often less about what I did and more often about bringing healing to other people. Hearing the call at each stage was essential, but it was more critical to feel the call in my gut and chest.

Retire had to become *inspire* ... or it would not last.

2

Affirming Growth

Among the Young, the Old, and the Disenfranchised

With young Lasallians at Lewis University outside Chicago

Senior Lasallians Missionaries at Coming Home workshop (2019)

Calling voters in Wisconsin and Georgia

For several years after retirement, I volunteered with the national Lasallian Volunteers office and visited these young men and women in cities throughout the US.

I affirmed the good I observed, shared some teaching ideas to improve their work with youth, and learned a lot myself in the process. Whether I was sitting in

Lasallian Volunteers Jen and Andy at their 2005 wedding

the back of a classroom, standing on the sidelines of soccer practice, or joining a counselor visiting the homes of her clients, my travels made me realize how much I was gaining from this beautiful experience of affirming young people. (It has even brought me many invitations to weddings, baptisms, and graduations). It is family. It feels good. It is one way I have continued "doing" in retirement.

Another way I continued "doing" was in being part of the leadership team of the Christian Brother's District of Eastern North America. For six years, I visited our Brothers throughout the northeast to learn how they were managing their lives, their mission to society, and their local community.

I had particular responsibility for elderly Brothers—a large number of men my age and above. I learned a lot from listening to their experience, and I loved coming up with short weekend workshops that allowed them to share their wisdom with others.

I quickly realized my enthusiasm to create the series I called "DENA Connect" was also a deep need I had within myself. The titles included: Wounded Healer, Lasallian Spirituality in the Golden Years, Thinking Out of the Box, Healing Touch, the Third Age, Reiki, Aging Process, and Coming Home.

The year 2020 was a critical election year in our country. The management of our pandemic response, emerging racism, questioning the rule of law in our country, and the apparent slide toward authoritarianism prompted me to work on encouraging my fellow citizens to vote.

I chose to help the swing state of Wisconsin, the city of Milwaukee in particular, through the organization called Common Ground WI.

Along with about 20 others, I met with a Common Ground organizer on a Zoom video call three times a week for training, which was followed by hours of phoning disenfranchised voters who needed help getting to the polls or voting absentee. The record-breaking voter turnout for the November election was proof of success.

The experience inspired me to sign up to help voters in Georgia for the special runoff elections in early January 2021. I was part of a large community-based organization that contacted millions of citizens via door knocking, postcard mailings, and phone calls. Citizens in Georgia were receptive to my calls. The homebound effort gave me a little peace in a toxic political environment amidst a dangerous health crisis.

I had taken the opportunity of staying at home for most of the year 2020 to be of help to the administrators of our Brothers in the northeast.

This ranges from being on committees and developing programs for elderly Brothers to regularly contacting certain ones to inquire about their wellbeing.

The aging process among these men has brought to light the challenge of dementia. We need professional help in assisting our members and coaching those who want to help members with dementia. As lifelong teachers dedicated to logic and learning, we find it hard to deal with dementia. Monthly workshops led by experts help to bring us to a better understanding of the issues and motivation to adopt more helpful approaches.

Br. Bill and I joined Lasallian Volunteers Jacquie, Matt, and Becca upon completion of graduate school.

3

Collaboration in
a Changing World

The Eagle and the Condor

With time, Lasallians will embrace both
condor thinking (heart and mystical) and
eagle thinking (brain and material).

For the Lasallian Family, the big question today is this: to what extent has the universe—that surrounds us and calls us Lasallians—changed dramatically, challenging us to keep up, engage, and ultimately use it to further our mission in the world?

Those in the third half find this question challenging because they remember the past successes and are slow to realize the rapid change in our present world.

Today, our universe is wrapped in the mystery of inclusion, co-responsibility, and leadership from the ground up. It is a significant change in the way we think of ourselves, and it was predicted for our time in the prophecy of the eagle and the condor.

This legend, originating in the Andes Mountains of Peru, states that human societies divided and took different paths throughout history.

Some went the way of the condor—representing the heart, intuitive and mystical. Others went the way the way of the eagle—representing the brain, rational and material.

In the 1490s, the prophecy said the two paths would converge and the eagle would drive the condor to the edge of extinction. And so it did with the Spanish Conquistadors, the World Wars, and the economic domination by the north.

Fast forward 500 years later and a new epoch would begin—one in which the condor and the eagle would have the opportunity to reunite and fly together in the same sky along the same path. This began in the 1990s. If the condor and eagle accept the opportunity, they would create a most remarkable offspring unlike any we've ever seen before.

We can take the prophecy of the condor and the eagle at many levels.

The standard interpretation is this: it foretells the sharing of indigenous knowledge with the technologies of science, the balancing of yin and yang, the bridging of northern and southern cultures, and the rise of the feminine to bring mindfulness to people and organizations. It's about balance, inclusion, oneness, and peace. (It sounds to me like the Spirit of God hovering over the waters).

We can take the prophecy of the condor and the eagle at many levels.

However, the most powerful message it offers is about consciousness. It says that we have entered a time when we can benefit from the many diverse ways of seeing ourselves and the world, then use these as a springboard to higher levels of awareness. As human beings, we can truly awaken and evolve into a more conscious species.

I can recall my feeling of empowerment when the Brothers' Superior General Álvaro Rodríguez Echeverría called for the refoundation of the Lasallian project in 2007. Intuitively, I understood he was advocating the radical renewal of our Lasallian enterprise to serve the needs of youth and families better today. I felt he was personally inviting every Lasallian to take part. He instinctively understood the family values of ownership, engagement, and appreciation. The word "passion" entered the Lasallian lexicon to describe association for the mission.

My favorite theory of change
for the Lasallian Family.

Refoundation always reminds me of the incredible transformation of the Church at Vatican II in the 1960s. Many of the old pigeons ensconced in the church steeples had to negotiate with some mighty new wings called condors.

Since the 1990s, there have been many examples of this transformation in our Lasallian world. They include:

✓ The growing use of the phrase "Lasallian Family"

✓ The emergence of Lasallian associative groups

Art: Brother Richard Buccin

✓ The hundreds of Lasallians who have learned to exert leadership in their mission

✓ The new, innovative intentional communities

It seems to me that the condor is most certainly rising.

In reminding the Lasallian world that more than 50% of its members are now women, Brother Álvaro Rodríguez Echeverría invited us to reflect on the "feminine face that the Lasallian enterprise has today."

This invite reaches far deeper than simply counting how many men and women there are. This feminine (condor) resides like the masculine (eagle) in the soul of each member of the family, whether they are male or female. I suspect Brother Álvaro was intimating that the balance in our Lasallian family has been seriously tipped toward the masculine for hundreds of years.

> The feminine (condor) resides like the masculine (eagle) in the soul of each member of the family.

If Carl Jung were alive, he might say this dramatic change in demographics should signal every member to generate more feeling to balance their thinking. Thinking simply organizes material from an objective standpoint, just as an engineer (eagle) might do. Feeling, however, organizes material from the perspective of what is essential to one's well-being, like a mother protecting her children (condor).

Since these represent different rational ways of organizing the same material, it is challenging to gain balance, especially in a Lasallian world dominated by eagle thinking for much of its history.

Similarly, Jung would encourage the practice of intuition to balance sensation. Sensation looks for patterns in what is present here and now (eagle). Intuition looks for how that explains what led to the current state of affairs and how the situation may evolve (condor). It's all about balance.

Henry Regan offers a good example of how our eagle and condor thinking can move toward collaboration rather than conflict. Len Cariou plays Regan, the family patriarch and former New York police commissioner, on the hit TV drama Blue Bloods. He is in the third half of his life. His son Frank (played by Tom Selleck) is the current police commissioner. His grandchildren all work in various levels of the department or the district attorney's office (hence the title of the show).

Each week's scene captures the family around the dinner table in conversation that always gets around to issues in their daily lives. Enter Henry, who still sits at the end of the table as the family's true patriarch. He loves his grandchildren and their families—these ties save him from being a genuinely grumpy older man.

Henry is quite aware that his opinion usually is not sought out, but this never stops him from wading into conversations. You can guarantee he will insert his dated police values such as being an opponent of gay officers on the force or treating mentally ill perpetrators as normal. And he simply won't take a stand that is contrary to the local pastor or the bishop.

Henry desires things to be as they were in the past, which again brings to mind Richard Rohr's "regressive restoration of persona." But what's redeeming about Henry is that he never leaves a dinner table discussion in a huff. He is a true grandpa (at 75 plus) and has a big heart. He engages all family members with a clear stand on everything, and each works on getting him to adjust his stance. The loving relationship they share often seems to melt his attitude and to get him to come around. He seems to grow a little with each discussion and, from time to time, he begrudgingly admits he doesn't have all the answers.

The Regan family circle is slowly converting him and helping him bring his vast treasure trove of life experience to bear on life today. He could be transformed by the end of the series into a genuine medieval blue blood, a remarkable human in touch with his deepest self that sets him apart from ordinary people.

It is easy for members of organizations like the De La Salle Christian Brothers to identify with Henry. They also contributed their lives to a worldwide organization's success and proudly feel they own the results. They think they are the face of the franchise. And though many of us at this age feel ignored now that we no longer have position and power, we stay at the table and respect, listen to, and depend on our younger Lasallians to help us balance our traditional insights with today's reality. The resulting balance is one that few others in our society are in a position to enjoy. It is where "doing" and "being" meet in the third half of life.

These interactions often alter our opinions and attitude and can bring out hidden gold in each of us.

> The focus
> must be on our
> present universe,
> and dreams
> for our future
> must outnumber
> memories.

Wisdom is another word for this gold. Change is constant. The focus must be on our present universe, and dreams for our future must outnumber memories.

All realize that change is a constant on this journey and a sign of God alive with us. We respect the divinity in ourselves and all people as we champion issues such as ecological sustainability, just policies, immigration, social justice, fair distribution of wealth, racial justice, non-violence, and women's rights.

Henry has ideals and wants to make the world a better place; I pursue high or noble principles and like to see things as they might or should be rather than as they are.

On the healing side, I am highly compassionate and empathetic to others' needs and seek to bring peace, health, and attention to friends and society. I value harmony and integrity in human relationships but often find these values to be out of step with the rest of the world's more concrete pursuits. I am usually attracted to those whom others have overlooked seeing the positive qualities that lie beneath the surface.

Healers are good listeners and put people at ease. I believe the experience of being listened to is the closest to being loved. I do not like conflict and go to great lengths to avoid it. I place little importance on who is right and who is wrong in such situations, and focus on how conflict makes people feel. It's a trait that can make anyone appear irrational and illogical.

Put another way, my life has been about kindness. What I expect from others is simply what I wish to give them in return.

Today, in my third half, I have focused on simpler yet significant kindness. I walk for two miles in the early morning, and greet everyone I pass with a "good morning," a practice seldom seen with strangers in New York City. For me, it's a simple connection with my neighbors and a way of welcoming the light of a new day. In no way is it a quid pro quo for their kindness. But after several months of saying hello, a fair number of my neighbors returned my greeting with a "good morning to you."

I work from my third floor bedroom where I have a full view of Marion Avenue in the Bronx. One day I observed a police officer writing a parking ticket for a car illegally parked in front of our house. Without hesitation, it took me only a few minutes to write a handwritten note to the car's owner.

> Sorry for your troubles.
> Hope this might help a little.

I left it on the windshield and included some money.

Responses to situations like this well up within me often, and I expect they are simply a desire to do for others what I would want them to do for me.

This is the meaning of kindness, and it must come from a God place within us.

PART II

Being
in the
Third Half

My Third Half is filled
with opportunities to grow
and BE good for others.
It is a process of becoming,
living out what I
<u>am</u> meant to be.

I appreciate Godness in nature.

I cherish God's revelations in my dreams.

I am in love with Anima.

I delight in Mary's embrace of mystery.

I travel far in the Spirit without leaving home.

*In the Yin Yang the former stands for night, unknown, softness, and inward energy . . . the **BEING** of my retirement*

4

Befriend the Earth in Godness

Exhilarating was the best word
to describe the sensation of the hurricane
passing right through my body.

In the fall of 2011, a few years into my third half, a hurricane helped me understand the Spirit within me.

It was late August when Hurricane Irene began moving through the northeast toward Canada, and I was staying at Stevenson Hall in Narragansett, Rhode Island. I decided to step outside and feel the gale force winds and rain pounding against me.

Exhilarating was the best word to describe the sensation of the hurricane passing right through my body without resistance or harm. In that moment, I was one with nature moving all around me. What most caught my attention was the large, graceful trees on the front lawn swaying passionately in a wild orchestrated dance.

In my deepest self, I identified with those trees and realized how close God was in the wind and rain and the heavens beyond. Trees always seem to be low on any ego concerns and high on modeling a great open stance in their creator's presence. Deeply loved and cared for, I root myself in this earth and stretch out to connect with my Creator God.

> I root myself in this earth and stretch out to connect with my Creator God.

Seldom do I see one tree alone in a field. Generally, they are together in a stand or forest. Their beauty and strength are enhanced as they reach together for the sky.

I am a part of a Lasallian forest of 90,000 others who live, grow, and praise God together and by association. I believe God has a special love and affection for this group.

Together we seek God, together we find God, together we are God to others—the disenfranchised of this world—and they are God to us. It is one big circle of life jointly working out our salvation by laying down our lives for one another. Prayer is sitting in awe of this circle.

It is not so much that God has a plan for us as much as it is that God has set in motion a sacred process of enhancing life in our world. We need only accept the surprises, embrace the paradoxes with compassion, and allow the spirit to inspire. Kindness everywhere is the result.

This sacred process reminds me of findings is physics a few years ago. The Nobel Prize was given to Peter Higgs for the Higgs Boson, the most basic building block of the universe that forms the world we know today. He called the boson "the God particle" and, despite his later denials, the term stuck with every news outlet —and especially with me.

For some time I have imagined God to be the energy at the subatomic level that gave and gives being to everything that lives—the essence of everything and the Spirit of God unfolding in our world.

People, places, and situations provide a more personal encounter with God. I hear, see, feel, and intuit a *presence* that connects love within me with love out there. Could it be that God within connects with God without? God is the depth dimension in solitude, friendship, community, death and hope. I want to hold these moments forever.

The best I can do is sit with the experience and be grateful.

5

Meeting the Spirit

God's Forgotten Language

Mandala:
My spiritual presence in all of creation.

Throughout my life, I have always helped people who ask. One day in 2007, Brother Dennis Lee said to me, "Ed, there are electrical problems at Ocean Rest and we moved the summer retreat to Pennsylvania. Can you pick up the retreat director at Newark airport and drive her out to Malvern?" And my dutiful reply? "No problem, Dennis!"

Close friends know this response from me is anything but that. I say it when three people want to use our community car and simultaneously go in three different directions. It is what I say after learning that our community sewage system has just backed up into our garage. In general, "no problem" means I have no idea how to handle the situation right now, but give me a little time and I will figure this out.

In the case of our retreat director, I understood her name was Felicia McKnight, that she was coming from Santa Cruz, California, and that she was a Jungian Spiritual Director. My "no problem" really meant, Where in the world is Malvern? What does this retreat director look like? And, maybe most importantly, How do I carry on a conversation from Newark, New Jersey to Malvern, Pennsylvania (a two-hour drive on a good day) with a Jungian Spiritual Director?

Most often, such challenging situations that inconvenience me have a hidden blessing—as it was that June afternoon in 2007 at Newark Liberty International Airport, the first day of a relationship that changed me forever and led to the most profound meaning in my third half of life.

Felicia seemed to be the only person waiting at arrivals that afternoon, making it serendipitously simple to locate her. Our conversations on the way to Malvern were surprisingly enjoyable. I heard about her family, her connection with the

> **Felicia questioned me to surface greater detail of my ideas and experiences.**

Brothers in Narragansett, and her parish work as a religion coordinator. I shared my challenge of preparing to transition from Highbridge and my hope to begin a new position with Lasallian Volunteers, as well as my rich experience with the families of the South Bronx.

Felicia really listened to me carefully. She made connections between various comments I made. She questioned me to surface greater detail of my ideas and experiences. She did not hesitate to share from her own experience but was so different from the many people I know who seem to move to their own expertise and agenda rapidly after I begin to share an idea. I could feel she wanted to learn more about me. I enjoyed the lengthy car ride and looked forward to spending the retreat days with her. In the days that followed I suspected that she might self identify as a spiritual director and if so I wanted to be one also.

Here with Felicia at the Spiritual Direction Internship.

Principal among my memories of that Malvern retreat was writing down dreams after having given up for several years, painting mandalas (circular symbols of the sacred), and sharing personally with the other participants.

On the last day of the retreat, I felt so freed through the workshop that I got a little carried away. During a special prayer involving watercolors, I invited the participants (three men) to paint a mural on my belly above the spot where I would lose a piece of my colon during surgery a week later. (Everyone hesitantly placed a little mark, but weren't feeling the freedom of mind I found).

In the months that followed, the Brothers leadership team of the LINE district invited Felicia to lead and direct the first ever Spiritual Direction Internship. Both she and they asked me to be among the seven founding participants, all men near the end of the second half of their lives. It was strange territory for me—a place I never envisioned myself earlier in life.

The internship was a series of ten weekends over a year and a half to learn the knowledge and skills required to be a spiritual director. Presentations were given each day by Felicia on depth psychology and spirituality—a big help for me as someone who never took a course in psychology. Each of us would take turns to lead a discussion on the book assigned for each weekend. Finally, each of us would meet with a directee (a person willing to converse with us about their experience of life and spirit) between the weekends and write verbatims of those meetings to be shared with Felicia in our supervision sessions on the weekends.

We Nobles (named after our meeting place on that street in Narragansett) met for the first time on Friday evening, January 11, 2008. I was about as articulate that evening about how I got to that point as I might have been with the same question on August 27, 1940 (the day I was born). I mumbled a few comments about the course helping me relate to people but had no idea. I was in the presence of Mystery.

This internship was like nothing I had ever experienced before. I was changing in ways I never planned and realized a new perspective for what was to be the third half of my life. I felt relieved, enlightened, encouraged, and affirmed. The entire internship was altogether one big surprise to me.

I was particularly moved by Jung's understanding of dreams as a window into my "being" or unconscious. For several years before the internship, I had been in the habit of waking and writing down my dreams, with little or no way of interpreting their meaning. Now I had Felicia and The Nobles to share them with and nurture some personal wholeness.

The Nobles
Named for the retreat house on
Noble Street in Narragansett

Ever since the end of the Spiritual Direction Internship in May 2009, I have continued seeing Felicia McKnight for spiritual direction—several times in person but mostly over the phone.

In preparation for these meetings, I send her my dreams at about six-week intervals. I often have insights into their meaning for my life, but I am always anxious to hear the wisdom from her years of experience being a Jungian Spiritual Director.

I am convinced that my dreams are theatre created by my unconscious or deepest self for the benefit of my conscious self. The message is not always straightforward because it is theater, which is why I need her help. The personal blessings here are to allow my conscious and unconscious to balance, to communicate, and to be at peace with each other.

My dreams reveal to me the values that I hold for myself in the deepest part of my being.

Following are good examples of this from the introductory sentence of my dreams, journaled over an eighteen month period.

March 1, 2020

Working with a team of researchers on food and food security. They related well with each other and were very professional in their talk and in their writing. I can see their research online.

April 30, 2020

In a leadership group for a union. The union is of one mind on most issues, but many of us are concerned about our spokesperson and whether he/she is really strong and on target.

May 12, 2020

I was part of a group of leaders that reviewed how we as a society could respond to a disease or pandemic present in many major cities and towns. I listened to all the ideas and outlines of plans and kept rather quiet. I went home thinking it all over and decided to help. I had done similarly in the past.

June 3, 2020

There was a group of adults linked together on the internet and they have the purpose of helping one of them psychologically. Each person regularly wrote to help the person. I am watching from the outside and concerned that each person does all that is necessary to get their comments all the way to the person.

June 4, 2020

Helping a group of young people to be their best by sharing meaningfully in discussions.

August 17, 2020

Was asked to be on a committee at school to get the most out of a few scholarships that were available to our students to go to college.

October 25, 2020

I was some kind of administrator/director of a medical team at some hospital or facility. I was strong on the concept that all admins should see the good the team is doing, respect where they are in their development, and realize they can not go faster than they are capable of right now.

Christmas Day

Trying indefatigably to help a group of elderly ignored men and women to get the needed medical assistance they deserve. I was especially interested in keeping their portfolios up-to-date with the medical authorities.

January 16, 2021

Part of the preparation for a nonviolent protest.

March 15, 2021

Part of a team of about 5 or 6 people who were advising the postal service on how best to mail prescriptions to people, especially those who needed to take heavy narcotics.

June 3, 2021

I won the right in some kind of a contest to care for a beautiful race horse on days of important races. There was staff for the details but I was like the honorary chairperson for the horse. I could make suggestions on who met the horse that day, some diet ideas, and could accompany the horse with its staff on walks.

These revealing dreams have different details but in each I am part of a group indicating clearly that I am a team player who respects the opinion of the rest of the circle. I am generally in on important decisions and always willing to listen to the ideas from the group.

My Lasallian Family calls this value *Association* and has reserved it as the core value of the family in recent years. For this family, Association invites members to form communities in which we share our faith and respond to the needs of our world today—the raison d'etre of our Bedford Park Community. I often wonder if the deep desire in me to work with others to improve our world is not the universal Christ or Spirit within me that keeps me faithful all these years to the Lasallian mission.

Years ago, John Sanford wrote the book, Dreams: God's Forgotten Language.

He said it all.

God is present in all creation and therefore present in the deepest part of each of us—our unconscious. Dreams are the medium of communication between our unconscious and our conscious selves. So, if we "get" the language of dreams we are in communication with God. The Bible is full of great examples like Mary and Joseph's dreams.

After recording almost 500 dreams over 15 years and reflecting on them, I am more comfortable with myself, kind, vulnerable, peaceful, and in love with God.

6

Anima

The Keeper of All That is Tender

My rendering of my
lifelong dream friend Anima.

Robert Johnson says virtually all of a man's feelings—happiness, sense of worth, sense of value, and moods—are feminine, the keeper of all that is tender and precious in a man's life.

He is clear about dream characters, especially the feminine ones for men. The feeling function moves men to be gentle, patient, close to nature, ready to forgive, and in harmony with people and animals. For Johnson, feeling is the capacity to value or give worth to something. It is in dreams that we men realize this vital side of ourselves.

During the Covid-19 pandemic, "sheltering in place" was my opportunity to realize the significance of my dreams over most of my life. In focusing on the many women characters in these dreams, I realized they could be considered a single person who, over time, matures and ages in tandem with my own life.

I named her Anima, and she and I have deepened and renewed our love for one another through a long series of dreams. She is a beautiful part of my unconscious self.

We first met back in the day. It was 1977, and we stayed in touch until 1989. Our relationship grew thanks to the many challenging situations we encountered together. Keeping a journal throughout this relationship helped me remember details—the quotes below.

No matter your theory on dreams, this is my perspective on my inner self.

Back in 1977, the sight of Anima was so attractive to me that it was tough to converse with her. She was a bartender, and I tried to order a drink that she seemed to delight in telling me she didn't know how to make it. Soon after, I tried to convince her to join me on a boat ride. On another occasion, she wore a revealing bathing suit covering most of her body that resembled a mermaid. I imagined her taking people for a swim, and I wished she had paid more attention to me instead.

In the next few years, we kept in touch, but her life was filled with various traumas. First, she injured herself seriously after falling off a ladder. Next, she injured her hand so severely that she lost the use of her fingers temporarily.

Finally, we both thought she had a terminal illness. It made me realize what she meant to me.

I wrote at the time: "We wish her final days to be as happy as possible. I wanted to pay attention to any announcement she would make because she was an extraordinary person, especially about the world situation. She seemed to be very close to my way of thinking and seeing the world. She was rather distant, aloof, and not given to a lot of talk—shadowy, hazy." (Her terminal illness turned out to be a false diagnosis, thank God).

So much trauma. I was falling in love. We were young. Our lives were so busy. I just wanted to sit with her.

I remember writing: "On a backpacking trip, I was staying at some house or hotel, but she was at a youth hostel. One night I went to her place, and I wanted to talk to her alone, but some young people were there. The young people did not understand, so I could not talk one-on-one with her. Then, some youth supervisor came around and said it was time for bed and lights out. I had to leave and was frustrated at not being free to talk with her."

In the 1942 film Casablanca, Rick and Lisa took time apart from each other even though they loved deeply. Anima and I did the same—for almost 20 years!

In 2007, Anima and I crossed paths again.

She looked to be 19 or 20 years old. Her hair was now long and flowing past her shoulders. She wore a gown that made it easy to see the shape of her body. She said nothing, but I knew again she was made for me. I desperately wanted to learn more about her and what her life was like since we first met.

I wouldn't see her again until six months later, in January 2008, at a teachers' meeting.

In my journal, I recalled that she was "mature, smart, alert, beautiful, and the focus of my attention," as well as very helpful to the people around her at the meeting. I tried getting her attention by saying things I thought were funny. She was not impressed. I became embarrassed. With time, she forgave me, and our relationship grew.

A few years later, I wrote that she became "mysterious, quiet, and serious" and before long "simple, holy, humble, and always very attractive."

Sometimes, she would go over the edge on humility. I wrote in 2009 that she was "in such good shape after running a marathon, yet continually putting herself down. She had everything but was not aware of it."

Along the way, we shared some fantastic experiences, captured in my heart and recorded forever through the words in my journal. She has held many leadership positions in the social services field—always professional, calm, and results-orientated. I wrote that "while working in an assisted living facility, she cared for an elderly gentleman who had once been active and a leader in his field. Now he was forgetful. She was so patient with him."

She often sought very physically demanding jobs, from working in an auto body repair shop to, more recently, repairing boilers in shopping centers while enduring hot, noisy conditions. Amina was invited to dismantle a very difficult boiler. She was ready to go at it, goggles and all. "She is amazingly hardworking," I wrote. "Knowledgeable, delighted, and confident to be asked and chosen for the job."

She also has helped me write many proposals for different social service projects. Often she is met with criticism on her ideas, but she keeps trying. A recent project she embraced was organizing an event to celebrate my life. She was clear that she welcomed my thoughts for the event, but that she would be the final arbiter of the day.

One rather tense time for both of us was in 2010 when she gave birth to our child. We were a long distance away from any doctor or hospital, and I was the only help she had. My words that morning: "When the little one's head started to show, I wondered if I could help out, and decided instead to encourage Anima to push. And I helped a bit. A great relief to hear the cry of birth."

From time to time, her social conscience and big mouth got us in trouble. On one occasion, while in Syria, she was to be punished for speaking out in favor of women's rights. The authorities were going to cut the back of her hand. My apolitical words in my diary at the time were: "We were traveling through a foreign country not noted for its citizens' rights or fairness. She insists on pushing the bar on some behavior not allowed in that country. I cannot recall the nature of it. She gets caught, and they decide they will cut the back of her hand as a punishment. I'm not sure what effect it will have on her ability to use her hand, but I suspect it will cause her to lose its use. It takes me only a short moment to decide to offer my hand instead."

On a personal level, she is not afraid to admit she has limitations. A few years ago, she participated in a group discussion I ran. The following day I wrote:
"I asked the group to take some kind of psychological survey and, from the results, I could see that Anima had some area of her personality that needed work. I wondered if she was too full of herself to be able to realize she needed help. I felt unqualified to help her but knew where she could get help. I was agreeably surprised when she agreed to seek help for whatever she needed."

A short time later, we both were on a long hiking expedition and she was selected to be my coach for the trip. At the time I admired her simple, straightforward way of dealing with challenges—she knew what she was doing.

"At one point, I put my foot in cold water, like a stream, and immediately saw the water turn red. I had stepped on a hidden trap that closed on my foot and ankle. I could tell that only my veins were cut—not an artery, because the blood was not pulsating out of my foot. I was calm, and she knew exactly how to release the trap."

Of course, we have had our ups and downs over the years. Sometimes I've been a little late on being there for her. Other times I've tried a little too hard to help. Over the years, I've realized when to step up, and I have learned that love can often mean stepping back.

At least on one occasion we decided to get counseling together. It was my idea, and Anima surprised me by being open to it. In typical Anima style, she pointed out several personal traits she thought I needed help with.

"We had a counselor that understood my interests. He was good and helped me see things that Anima wanted me to understand. Sometimes I wondered if he was a little too understanding of her. After all, I was paying him. But I did realize he had my best interest at heart."

Our love for each other has spilled over into care and service to others. Often it takes the form of risk-taking. Recently, I tried to catch a train at the Metro-North 125th Street station in NYC when a missing section of stairs obstructed my way up to the platform. It was an opening through which a person could fall to the street. There was no other way up to the train. Other passengers were nearby. Another man and I stepped across the opening and helped others do the same. Much to my surprise, the last person we helped was Anima. I had forgotten her plan to catch a train that day. As she began to cross the expanse with our help, I put my hand on her back and could feel the heat and sweat of nervousness through her clothes. I realized for the first time that her movements were labored and she seemed a bit frail. I greatly admired her willingness to take the risk of bridging the gap

Modern Holy Family

and accepting our helping hand. It turned out well for all of us, but my thoughts on that train ride mainly were on how Anima and I have aged as we have enjoyed each other.

These are but a few glimpses of my love affair with Anima, drawn from my memory and my dream journal.

Like Casablanca, I have often said to my Anima the Bogart line, "Here's looking at you, kid." In the movie, Rick and Lisa are physically separated by war events but will never be so in their hearts.

Similarly, Anima and I will never be separated by anything because she is my dream. She visits me at night from the deepest recesses of my unconscious. She is as real as those angels who visited Joseph and Mary to advise their "yes."

I am reminded of Anima and our baby every time I visit the retreat house in Malvern, PA. On display under the chapel's altar is *A Quiet Moment*, a sculpture by Timothy Schmalz depicting the Holy Family. An olive wood sculpture called Modern Holy Family similarly reminds me of my inner self.

In both, the Joseph figure dominates the work. It catches my eye each time I enter the chapel. At first, I thought the artists exaggerated the importance of the Joseph figure by his size and protective stance. The Mary figure seemed a bit more demeaned than my impression of her from scripture.

Over time I realized a whole new personal insight into the sculptures.

First, with Joseph and Mary I am reminded of the balance between the masculine and feminine within me. It is another yin and yang reminder for me in the balance and harmony of the feminine and masculine energies in my life—the giving and receiving in life.

Secondly, the child reminds me of the new life that emerges from me each day in retirement. It is a delicate energy that needs to be nourished, cared for and affirmed by myself and others.

Lastly, I am the Joseph who protects, cares for, and listens to my feminine feeling side hidden deep within me represented by the Mary figure—also called Anima. Likewise, both Mary (Anima) and I nurture the new life we bring into the world.

A Quite Moment

7

My Magnificat

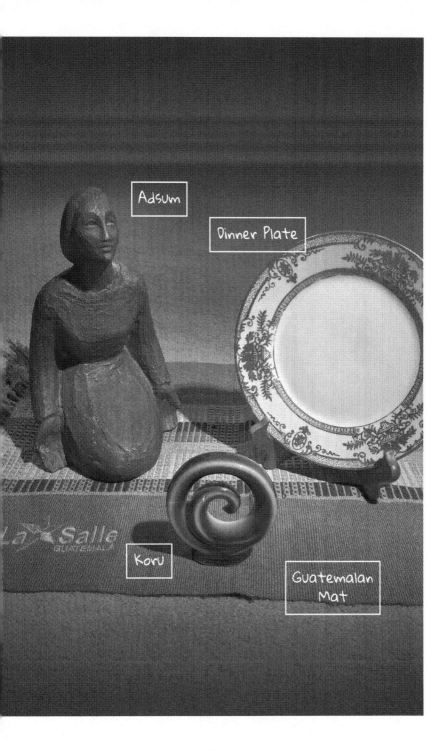

Adsum

Dinner Plate

Koru

Guatemalan Mat

My experience with dreams and inner life is on display daily in my bedroom. Gone to the closet are all the diplomas, awards, and charts of the first and second half of life. They have been replaced by beautiful art I have created, symbols of some of my dreams, a place for yoga, and a unique floor-level configuration—a feminine incarnation.

The latter rests on a small woven mat from Guatemala, embossed with the word Lasallian in one corner, and includes:

- ✓ One gypsum statue, named Adsum, of a kneeling woman looking up with hands open to the sky
- ✓ One dinner plate, trimmed in gold leaf
- ✓ One ceramic Koru, the national symbol of New Zealand

Their meaning for me has changed with the seasons of my life, but generally today they represent the following:

Adsum (I Am Here)

The statue has traditionally reminded me of Mary's response to the angel's invitation in her dream. The openhanded posture of this woman is receptive. With time and thought of Mary's deep love for her God and vice versa, I began to see the feminine face of God—the free, unlimited, unrestricted love that God has for me. More recently, it reminds me of my feminine side emanating from my deepest self. "I am here" is my response to people, places, things, and all creation around me—to God's presence everywhere.

I feel the pull away from the competitive, individualistic, non-contemplative world we live in to be more relational and mutually empowering in my interactions. This feminine within me helps me shift away from the global paradigm of dominance and individualized salvation and toward a collective awakening and service to all beings. In Lasallian terms, this is the deepest level of association—the emergence of the feminine within each of us and our collective body.

"The most precious gift we can offer others is our presence. When mindfulness embraces those we love, they will blossom like flowers." Thich Nhat Hanh

Gold Leaf Dinner Plate

If adsum is my stance in the world, then the gold-edged plate—one of the last remaining of Mom's "good china"—is a constant reminder of the gold within me, the value and goodness in my deepest self. It is my heart set on God.

Earlier in life, I believed I could build up that gold by practicing good works or doing traditional spiritual exercises. It is clear now that the gold is there due to the love and giftedness of being created a human and is not dependent on my efforts. Using that love in practice in the world is one way to grow. We Lasallians do this together and call it "Association for the Mission."

The Koru

In 2017, while attending the International Symposium of Lasallian Women in Auckland, I discovered the Koru. Its spiral shape reminds me of how my life journey circles and gently moves toward my God center as I grow through my life seasons.

On another level, I feel the centrifugal movement of being sent by that center back out into the world.

Everlyn Ontono of De La Salle Secondary School, Bomama, PNG, attended the International Symposium of Lasallian Women in Auckland.

Guatemalan Mat

The mat upon which the symbols rest is my Lasallian Family. It is the extended worldwide networks of adults and children touched by the mission.

Almost daily, I stand or sit before this feminine incarnation and quiet myself with several deep breaths. I notice the plate's gold and the Koru's spiral, but most often, I stay with the Adsum. For me, it captures Mary's "yes" to the invitation of the dream angel, and I want to imitate her. Gabriel invited her to be the mother of Jesus. She questioned and then said "yes." The angel promised her the Holy Spirit and the power of the Most High. He did his job and was never seen again.

Mary elaborated on her "yes" in her Magnificat.

I have taken Eugene Peterson's translation of Mary's Magnificat and added my own heartfelt praise and prayer.

"And I say I'm bursting with God-news;
I'm dancing the song of my Savior God."

> *Early most mornings or traveling by car or subway, I imagine God saying to me "I love you" and after holding that breath for a few seconds, I exhale with "I love You." I am so grateful to be alive, alert, and healthy enough to be in love with You. I enjoy singing the praise of friends and strangers for their efforts to help and connect with people everywhere. All of this is You emerging through me. I am the mirror of your exuberance in your creation. In another way, it is where your deep gladness in me and the world's deep hunger meet. I realize this God-news also includes the sufferings, troubles, and challenges that can awaken in me a benevolent and compassionate heart despite everything to the contrary.*

"God took one good look at me and look what happened—I'm the most fortunate person on earth!"

> *I have family and friends who support and challenge me. I have survived several auto accidents that could have easily left me very limited in body and mind. I have thrived as a resident of the most dangerous neighborhoods in NYC. As an EMT I helped several women deliver their babies at home and on their front lawn. The courage to be this is You who resides in my most profound self, way deeper than ego or persona. I have never deserved this good fortune. I want only to use it in the love of You.*

"What God has done for me will never be
forgotten, the God whose very name is holy,
set apart from all others."

> *What I have done in life has been your Dream for me
> developing in my imagination—never near perfect
> but always an effort to please You, my lover. Anything
> I am reflects You, like the lilies, roses, daffodils,
> trees, ocean, newborn babies, and aging seniors.
> After all, you made me a reflection of yourself. I am
> honored to bring Lasallians together to learn, share
> and praise; to live with young, gifted Lasallians;
> and help your most vulnerable people.*

"His mercy flows in wave after wave
on those who are in awe before him."

> *The thought of You reminds me of my limitations,
> shortcomings, and dismal performances.
> These memories no longer separate us, but I'm
> starting to understand my weaknesses are my greatest
> strengths in our relationship. Deep within me is your
> glory. It is your name written in me. Help me to
> behold it. It's the proper order of our creation.*

"He bared his arm and showed his strength,
scattering the bluffing braggarts."

> *You protect and care for me and all creation, perhaps
> not in the way my ego wants and the time frame
> I desire but according to the Plan. I trust.*

"The starving poor sat down to a banquet;
the callous rich were left out in the cold."

> *You reverse the world's strengths and powers in favor
> of the poor, weak, and those who know they need
> you. I now realize if roles were reversed for all the*

time, talent, and energy I have shared with low-income families, I would be welcome and supported. And I have had something to share only by accident of birth. We are all brothers and sisters in one family. In these covid times in our country, I am becoming more aware of the deep divide based on economic levels. Help me to help heal.

My Gabriel in retirement has been a Charlie Angel. One night in 2016, shortly after his death, my old friend and former colleague Charlie Kitson sent me an email in a dream:

New message	_ □ ×
To	Ed
From	Charlie

Step back and get the big picture.
See the direction God wants. Don't be
thrown off or distracted. Review, refresh,
be courageous against odds. Remember
not to fall into the trap of any negativity.
Our very weaknesses are our strengths.

I had no questions. I agreed with every word. It was clear to me that Charlie was my deepest self, communicating a very profound message to my conscious self about the third half of my life. It is about being in love with God. It is about courage, focus, and balance. It is about the humility and the poverty of being an authentic human being. It is the way I want to live and be and do. It is not easy to practice, but it is where my soul is these days.

8

Imagine the Road Ahead

Pilgrims: Day one, a few feet from the Pacific.

Over the years, I have realized that my life is a journey. I feel like Ulysses and others who often returned home after the wars only to set out on another trip.

About a year after the Spiritual Direction Internship lead by Felicia McKnight, I joined a group of young Lasallians on a bike ride from Oregon to New Jersey to raise awareness of the Lasallian mission.

This two-month trek opened my eyes to a broader understanding of my life journey; I realized I was on a pilgrimage. Not to some shrine but to live each moment with intention. I called my 19 companions on the ride "pilgrims."

I wrote about them at the time: "Pilgrims embrace change, balance life and death, befriend the earth, wrestle with dragons, live in the now, receive hospitality, be family, serve neighbors, discover personal gold, and love God everywhere." It is a simple and meaningful way to be in the third half of life.

Pilgrims are never alone. They walk in the presence of God, experienced within themselves, in others, and the beauty of creation. This presence is the softness, warmth, and gentleness that validates my masculine world. It is an empathetic, value-based, feeling "heart" that intuitively knows life's practical wisdom.

This presence is the tenderness, compassion, understanding, and even wildness that makes it harder and harder to judge people, get excited about TV football games, or cheer for consecutive life sentences for criminals.

The presence is never weak or merely emotional. It is as strong as Mary, His mother, and many of the women in the Greek myths like Psyche. I think it is the feminine face of God, called Sophia by many.

Pilgrims put aside the pursuit of perfection. I'm now a student of the spirituality of imperfection. My wounded, limited, screwed-up human condition is the perfect stance before God. The Spiritual Direction Internship taught me that the human condition is pure gold when relating to my fellow humans—and through them to God. I can be proud of being a link between creation here below, and the gods above in my imperfection.

Therese of Lisieux once said: "If you are willing to bear serenely the trial of being displeasing to yourself, then you will be for Jesus a pleasant place of shelter."

Since the bike ride, pilgrimage has meant more than a walk or ride with others from one place to another. It is no longer a straight line. It is somewhat circular and spiral-like. I can be on a pilgrimage and never leave home or neighborhood. My progress in life moves more gently and indirectly toward the center, the endpoint, or God.

Of Labryinths

I discovered the Labyrinth and realized it is an excellent symbol for me, just as it has been for centuries for pilgrims in the great cathedrals of Europe.

My life path seems to be most like the labyrinth, with its approach shifting in unexpected ways, sometimes diverting me from my goal but ultimately showing me the way toward growth, life, and God.

I am not alone while prayerfully walking the path. With me are all the Lasallian partners I have known and worked with in life; the young women and men I have lived and walked with in community; and the De La Salle Brothers.

At most times, progress is moving one circuit closer to the God center, but soon, the labyrinth drops me back a circuit or two—an ebb and flow that gradually moves forward to the center just like in real life.

God at the center of my labyrinth has changed in much the same way any lover changes. Early on, Jesus was a magician who could change the world as he did with the loaves and fishes. Then Jesus was a Messiah who was to be obeyed... or else. Then Jesus was fully human and fully divine, and it was up to me to use my energy to bring about His reign.

More recently, I am called to discover the divinity in myself and others.

In the third half of my life, I have become more aware of the Universal Christ found everywhere and in everything. Creation is more important than ever. I can commune with God as God. This is the wisdom of this part of my life.

PART III

Onward

My Third Half is filled
with opportunities
to grow and change
the world around me.

I imagine my life.

I model the way.

I inspire a shared vision.

I challenge the process.

I enable others to act.

I encourage the heart.

9

Living with
Intention

Like Mary and Elizabeth, I can change
the world with "yes" to my angels.

The New Testament discusses many women who gave birth under challenging circumstances. Each was filled with human questions and human willingness. Mary, Elizabeth, Anna, and others showed incredible wisdom in saying yes to God's plan for the new life they were to bring into the world.

I call their attitude charismatic leadership—the ability to connect with people deeply. They remind me of my need to say yes at this point in my life.

Early on in retirement, I had a remarkable dream one night in April 2009 that recalled the women in the New Testament. I recorded it in the morning in my dream journal:

> "I HAD A SENSE OF GLEE AND PRIDE IN TELLING SOME FRIENDS THAT I WAS PREGNANT.
> THEY SEEMED TO ALSO BE EXCITED. I FELT MY ABDOMEN AND COULD DETECT A SLIGHT BULGE.
> I HAD NO CONCERN IN THE DREAM ABOUT THE STRANGENESS OF THIS SITUATION.
> ONLY EXCITEMENT."

Similarly, I assisted my Anima in giving birth in another remarkable dream in December 2010.

Both instances tell me that I am pregnant with new life in my third half. The meaning that women find in physical birthing can point us toward the ways in which the transcendent is unfolding itself within the whole of our lives. Like the women of the New Testament, listening leads to action. I need to listen very carefully to God deep within myself, to struggling families in the world around me, and all of creation. No other way exists to understand another person than to listen to them. A talker learns little, but a listener learns so much. Lovers listen carefully. The whole notion of vocation presumes a deep sense of listening.

And like the women of the New Testament, listening leads to action. It is a form of leadership that calls me to imagine, model, inspire, challenge, and enable life in those I touch. This leadership is not derived from being elected or chosen, but simply from being an authentic human. There is no time to wait to be discovered, only time to be it and do it. It is a dream becoming.

IMAGINE

I imagine my life in terms of love and service—to love God and help my Lasallian Family be its best. It is all in the context of love. It is so simple. It is like breathing. It calms my spirit. It sets my compass. It is very humble. I am in love with God. I belong to God. I am God in this world.

Anything I do helps to bring about God's reign in our world. It is a mystery.

At the same time, I am vulnerable and imperfect. God understands because God created me with limits, and God is in love with me. We are in love with each other. Our love grows and deepens with time. Carrie Underwood sings "Just as I am, I come to Thee."

My ideal of service is to participate in whatever way I feel I can within Lasallian circles of women and men.

It might involve working together with needy families and individuals to bring significant positive change in their lives, family, and community. It's our mission in the world. My desire to serve emerges from deep in my heart. I like to think love has overwhelmed me to put out enormous energy for these circles and go way beyond my ego concerns.

I imagine how weaknesses, failures, and discouragements allow me to grow in love and service. In some way, they provide me collateral beauty—the search for meaning in heartbreak and disappointment. It's about love being in the middle of suffering, pain, and loss. Deep down, I believe what doesn't kill me makes me stronger. I am not good at this but I can, at least, see the possibilities.

Another service I offer is to continue helping and assisting our senior Brothers in enjoying their meaningful years in retirement and old age. By serving on committees, conducting workshops, and attending seminars, I can help design programs for these men.

MODEL

I can model the way of love and service in sharing my life and energy with my Lasallian Family in the Bronx. This involves sharing daily life activities with as many as five other Lasallians in this small family. It consists of affirming the actions of each at home and with the families they relate to in our neighborhood. It consists of radiating hope about the world. It shows how to accept aging and limitations, especially during the Covid-19 pandemic. It includes accepting my handicaps (including my limited hearing) and welcoming these handicaps as opportunities to move personal weaknesses into strengths.

An essential part of modeling the way is finding my voice by clarifying my values for the people I live and work with. I am not necessarily wanting them to be like me, but I would hope to see them demonstrate that we all are called to speak the truth—our truth. This is also an opportunity of aligning my actions with my values. It is the purpose of my website EdPhelan.com

Another way to model is to show younger people how to grow old gracefully. Never easy, but it is a much-needed mission in today's society. I can hope, pray, and do my best in all humility to let the joy within me shine forth.

INSPIRE

In speaking the truth, I can inspire a shared vision by imagining and ennobling possibilities for our family, our world, and ourselves.

In the third half, any power of position is gone.

I instinctively see and want to share ways of living in community at this time in history that will bring us together and do the greatest good for our world. We share ourselves in prayer and discussions, in breaking bread, by listening and responding, through disagreements, in smiles and hugs, and in dreaming of our future.

Our community in the Bronx is part of a network of other northeast US communities called the District of Eastern North America. As a province of the Christian Brothers, we share a rich history of hundreds of years of service to needy and poor youth begun in 17th century France. This inspired tradition is a huge blessing for the mission today, but it can limit how successfully the group responds to our current day's needs.

The center of this worldwide spiritual family in Rome has encouraged us to adjust our way of living according to today's needs and asks us not be overly influenced by the rich traditions of the past.

On the international, regional, and local level, this Lasallian Family searches for ways to change, grow, and improve their service to poor and vulnerable families. Old Testament-style prophets who can deeply love their tradition and simultaneously profoundly criticize it are needed in large numbers, for it is their deep love and passion that forces them to criticize their tradition.

CHALLENGE

The dualistic mind presumes that you don't love the family if you challenge the process. Wise prophets would say the opposite. Institutions prefer loyalists and "company men" to prophets. We're uncomfortable with people who point out our shadow or imperfections. However, it is these men and women who are the change agents of any organization.

In the US, these prophets in the Lasallian Family might:

- Encourage responsible boards of directors to recruit women for leadership positions in their schools and institutions such that their numbers might more closely resemble the percent of women in the Lasallian Family and in our society.

- Invite Lasallians to continually think out of the box to find new and creative solutions to the hardships of our day.

- Ask why a balanced racial mix of Lasallians is missing on many decision-making committees and councils.

- Inspire women and men, longtime Lasallians who I call Lifelong Lasallians, to organize themselves to be more effective change agents and visionaries of our future.

- Wonder why financially successful Lasallian institutions in the US do not commit substantial resources to the institutions that work directly with poor and vulnerable families in keeping with our family traditions and God's dream for humanity.

- Support the development of new, creative residential and non-residential Lasallian communities.

ENABLE

For many years I have admired these often-repeated words of Margaret Mead:

> "Never doubt that a small group of thoughtful, committed people can change the world. Indeed, it's the only thing that ever has."

I think of her words often when I see the opportunity to enable others to act. Change happened during the 2020 presidential election when I helped Common Ground call hundreds of Wisconsin voters. This small group, and others like it, helped turn Milwaukee (and consequently the state of Wisconsin) from red to blue.

Never doubt what a small group can do.

Developing many disparate relationships to bring change in our world speaks to me of radical hospitality—the practice of putting extraordinary effort and emphasis in making people feel welcome. This concept focuses on breaking down barriers that prevent people from participating in an action, campaign, or community. This is our attitude toward guests in our community on Marion Avenue in the Bronx. It's what drives my greeting to all of our neighbors on my early morning walks with a "good morning."

ENCOURAGE

I wish to encourage the heart. It is the appreciation of all the individual contributions to any project. It is celebrating the victory. It is creating a spirit of community, and it sets the stage for the group to take on even more significant change. Common Ground in Wisconsin invited all phone bank participants to gather online to celebrate the victory. It inspired me to seek a similar group in Georgia regarding the runoff election in January 2021. The subsequent record breaking turnout was a tribute to the large-scale organizing efforts to not only reach out to residents but also touch their hearts.

When I was the executive director of the Highbridge Community Life Center, six women residents of our community came to meet with me in my office. They explained that they wanted to have the potholes on their street filled to improve safety for their children. After a lot of discussion, the group decided to decorate the potholes for Halloween with funny and scary faces, then published photos in a local newspaper. The result was a parade of eight semitrucks full of asphalt delivered by the city in the days following the article. This experience firmly convinced the women they should celebrate the victory and move on to other things that were more difficult to achieve. Soon they were getting the city, and even the state of New York, to contribute millions of dollars to improve education in their local schools. They became a significant force to be reckoned with in the Highbridge community for years to come.

All of us humans can birth a new world daily as we

Imagine, Model, Inspire, Challenge, Enable, and Encourage.

In the end,
nothing changes
unless we

PART IV

The Bigger Picture:
A Cosmic Story

My Third Half is filled
with opportunities to
grow and realize
I am part of
the universe's story.

My story.

Our story.

The story.

There is a big picture
here that expands my
three halves boundary,
overlapping domes
that include:

my story,

our story,

and the story.

There is a big picture here that expands my three halves boundary. Richard Rohr describes it as three overlapping domes—my story, our story, and the story. His inspiration came from Joseph Pearce, who called these three overlapping spheres The Cosmic Egg.

My Story

Early on, my story was about my choice of schools, profession, and way of life. It was about me and what I made out of my life. I developed a self concept of achievement in difficult and challenging circumstances in the Bronx. I called it the first half of my life. It was my story developing and I had a lot to learn.

Our Story

Our story includes my story and significant relationships, *the us*—my family, coworkers, and team. For me, it is the Lasallian Family, and much like the second half of life.

Our story reminds me of a wall in our dining room that reads *What we love most about our home is who we share it with.* I hope that for many years to come, this community will be a meeting place for people of like mind to gather for sharing, support, nourishment, and reflection on how best to serve the needy and vulnerable families of the Bronx. It will be a home where neighbors and refugees are welcome, and a center for services to the surrounding community. As such, it will be a fantastic group of people who together will bring about the reign of God in our world.

The Story

Beyond my story and our story lives the story. The universe joins all our separate traditions and links all humans together. It is the Godness that permeates all of the created world. It is the transcendence we all seek in the third half. It is the big picture of all of our lives. It is the oneness that answers all the divisions in our world. Growing in this oneness is the blessing of the third half. It is holiness, the ultimate form of wholeness. I suspect we never quite get there in this life, but any effort toward this wholeness is a delight.

No wonder that Joseph Pearce called it the Cosmic Egg.

The story gets more simple as we age and grow. Personally, the story is the interconnectedness of all creation that I bring about by helping my neighbor. It's the call that flows from and enhances my love affair with my God. Any limitation I have only teaches me to put little trust in my ego concerns, and strengthens my confidence in the God of the creation all around me. I am part of the story.

Looking back over the eight-plus decades of my life, I honestly and humbly hope that my life might inspire and energize many others in our Lasallian Family and beyond.

And the story is changing my understanding of myself. As time goes on, I believe I am far more wonderful than I ever dared to imagine earlier in life.

I am more capable
than I ever dreamed …

because I am.

I am stronger than
my fears have allowed …

because I am.

I am genuinely more unique and
memorable than I have ever allowed
myself to acknowledge …

because I am.

Life ahead is staying afloat
on the Sea of Galilee with
calm sea, plenty of rocks,
and the Man who walks on it.

I am now wondering about the Fourth Half as I embrace the calm, crawl over the rocks, get in the boat, enjoy the company, and listen for the plan.

Thank you for reading My Third Half.
I hope you enjoyed or were inspired.

Our Bronx family in 2008.
Often a common realization for we Lasallians is
being part of a like-minded family, one that knows
how to balance the challenging work with a little fun.

MY JOURNEY TO THE THIRD HALF

FIRST HALF

August 27, 1940	Born in Brooklyn, New York
September 9, 1954	First day at La Salle Academy, New York (age 14)
September 1, 1958	Join the De La Salle Christian Brothers (age 18)
1963 - 1977	Teacher and principal in South Bronx (age 23-38)
October 1978 - June 1983	Campus Director, School of New Resources South Bronx Campus (age 38-43)

SECOND HALF

September 1983 - January 1, 2008	Teacher and Executive Director Highbridge Community Life Center Bronx, New York (43-67)

THIRD HALF

September 2008 - June 2013	Program Associate Lasallian Volunteers Washington, DC (age 67-73)
September 2013 - September 2017	Auxiliary Visitor, Leadership Team Brothers' District of Eastern North America (age 73-77)
October 2017 - May 2020	Director Senior Brothers Brothers' District of Eastern North America (age 77-80)
September 2, 2020 - January 1, 2021	Assist voters in Wisconsin and Georgia (age 80)

ABOUT THE AUTHOR

Ed Phelan has lived and worked in the Bronx, New York, for over 60 years as teacher, principal, college administrator, and executive director of a community agency.

Since high school, he has been a member of the De La Salle Christian Brothers, a religious order in the Catholic Church. Members of this group live and work in 80 countries across the world and, together with women and men partners, form the 95,000 strong Lasallian Family.

Ed retired on January 1, 2008, and has since used his lifelong energy by helping his neighbors, friends, and family, and by taking the time to reflect on the deeper meaning of life. He lives with other members of the Lasallian Family in the Bedford Park Community on Marion Avenue in the Bronx.

ACKNOWLEDGMENTS

Special thanks to Felicia McKnight,
Jungian Spiritual Director,
for the inspiration to write.

And a big shout out to Al Cassidy,
Literary Agent, for designing the book,
and helping me edit.